CONTENTS

Foreword

FELLOW MODELER:

What part of a model is most

SEEN - ADMIRED - and CRITICIZED?

— The Finish —

a fact which places painting as the most important final step in model making.

Early modelers built their models from scratch. If they painted their models, they had little or no choice in finishes as they were limited to the then available paints: house paint, enamels, artists' colors (which through thinning had to be adapted for small surfaces in order to be able to apply them). A model builder who obtained some prototype paint from a railroad shop considered himself lucky as this was "The McCoy" in *color match* (although this paint also had to be adapted).

The results, in general, were far from perfect—no model looked like its prototype, and the paints often blistered, peeled, chipped or cracked.

Today's modelers have many advantages unknown to early pioneers.

Today's modelers have a selection of numerous precision-made kits or ready-to-run, prepainted models, manufactured to scale.

Today's modelers also have available ready to use paints, formulated for *painting miniatures,* which can make a model appear finished and realistic, if properly applied.

Applicators also have been greatly improved—better brushes at lower cost, and spray applicators and air-brushes, unknown to early pioneers.

Despite the many improvements, some would-be railroaders (especially beginners) are of the opinion that all they need to paint *miniatures* is a brush (any old brush), and some paint (any old smear), . . . which magically arranges itself to a perfect finish. As this vain dream is never realized, finishing the model frequently remains unpleasant and everything is blamed for the modelers' failures except their own lack of information about paints—and their handling.

We know that if these modelers would spend a little time to study their projects (surfaces, paints and paint applicators) and accept simple guidance, they, too, would be able to get results which they could show with pride, and we believe that the sooner the modelers awaken to this reality, the sooner they will be on the right track to better looking models, easier painting and . . . more enjoyment.

1

We have for years received many inquiries from modelers, advanced as well as beginners, asking our advice in matters of painting models, which has prompted us to produce this manual as a guide for everyone who might be needing and looking for assistance.

We have chosen a simplified approach to our subject, from a new and different angle—which requires neither special knowledge nor experience.

By placing paint and its applications in a class with *mechanical* implements: hammers, pliers, screwdrivers, etc. (which most modelers handle easily), we would like to erase any confusion and doubts in the modelers' minds and replace them with confidence in the modelers' own *skill* and *ability* through their knowing:

1. What paint *IS*.

2. What paint *DOES*.

3. *HOW* it does it.

It is our hope that the information here presented, properly digested and applied, will equip the modelers on their journey into the world of color and enable them to explore their own roads, trails and by-paths.

Harald Rosenlund
FLOQUIL PRODUCTS, INC.
Cobleskill, N. Y. 12043

2

1. Why Miniature Paint?

When we speak about scale dimensions, we generally refer to the solid parts of the engines, cars, scenery, etc. The thickness of the coat of paint covering these parts either escapes attention or is taken for granted as being too thin or of no dimension to actually have any deciding effect on the appearance of the finished model. — These are misconceptions. —

We can show results—certain to surprise you—by applying a fixed thickness of paint to two surfaces of different scales:

$$1/5568'' = 1/64'' = 1\ 11/32''$$

Suppose we are looking at two *unpainted* engines

A—PROTOTYPE — Scale 1″

B—HO GAUGE — Scale 1/87″

IMPOSSIBLE! DEFIES BASIC RULES OF ARITHMETIC

Suppose we paint them with identical paint of identical thickness—1/64″ (which is very close to the average thickness of a coat of prototype paint).

When our paint has dried, we would expect the two engines to look alike except for size—*but they don't*—(an experience every modeler had who tried it).

WHY IS THIS SO?

Let us continue with our supposition. Suppose we—by some magic trick—were able to

A—*Reduce* our Prototype Engine into an HO Gauge Engine—and

B—*Enlarge* our HO Engine into a Prototype Engine.

First—what happens to our prototype (Scale 1″) engine?

To *Reduce* prototype, we must divide all dimensions by 87 (including our 1/64″ coat of paint):

$$1/64'' \div 87 = \frac{1}{64 \times 87}'' = \frac{1}{5568}''$$

—or in decimal, .00017959—roundly .0002″ (two ten-thousandths of an inch).

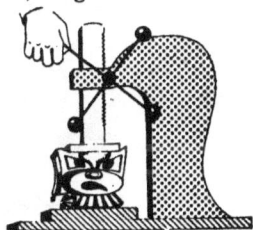

This is our prototype coat *REDUCED to HO* dimension, showing us that an HO scale coat of paint should be

LESS THAN TWO TEN-THOUSANDTHS OF AN INCH THICK.

For comparison—the thickness of the paper this is printed on is about .0035″ (three and one-half thousandths of an inch)—or 17.5 times thicker than our to-scale coat.

Now if we enlarge our HO engine to prototype size by *multiplying* all dimensions by 87 (including our 1/64″ coat of paint), here is what we would have:

$$1/64'' \times 87 = 87/64 = 1\text{-}23/64'' \text{ — or in}$$

decimal, 1.36″ (1.3593″).

The enlargement of our HO Gauge engine to prototype scale would increase our paint coat proportionately in thickness to more than an inch and a third: (1-23/64″) or 1-11/32″ *thicker* than its original thickness of the 1/64″.

1-23/64″ would bury or hide any surface projection smaller than this.

The figures we just established show a drastic difference in our original 1/64″ coat of paint, when applied to either:

A PROTOTYPE ENGINE—for which it was made and is suited—and if reduced to HO scale equals 1/5568″ (.0002″),

OR

AN HO ENGINE—for which it was NOT made and is NOT suited as it would equal a coating more than 1-1/3″ thick on a prototype engine.

THIS MAKES EINSTEIN EASY

Hence . . . 1/5568″=1/64″=1-11/32″

This leads us to only one logical conclusion:

MINIATURES REQUIRE MINIATURE PAINT

2. Changing Prototype Paint Into Miniature Paint

The following question is apt to come up. "Why don't we *reduce* prototype paint to miniature paint by using a thinner?"

We can *add* thinner to prototype paint, which naturally will *make it thinner* and perhaps easier to apply to a miniature surface, but *we can never reduce it to a miniature paint* because it is not "built" for this.

To explain this, we must first establish a few facts and features about paints, their ingredients and their main purposes.

Paint is a mixture of three main ingredients, each one having its own special purpose. Briefly the three ingredients, their characteristics and purposes are:

	INGREDIENT	CHARACTERISTICS	PURPOSES
A	PIGMENT	Finely granulated color particles.	Coloring, protection of surface.
B	BINDER	Gum-like, soluble resin.	Adhesion, gloss, protection of surface.
C	VEHICLE	Combination of liquids (thinners and solvents).	Makes application of A & B feasible.

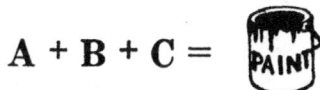

$$A + B + C = \text{PAINT}$$

By selecting, combining and grinding A, B and C, paint manufacturers can, within reason, produce paints for practically any purpose (for instance, prototype paint for prototypes, wall paint for walls, etc.).

We have seen that to be suitable for *miniatures*, a coat of paint should be *less than* .0002″ thick, which necessitates special processing—for instance:

1. *Reducing* the size of the pigment particles (to scale) through additional milling (grinding) and

2. *Selecting* suitable binders and vehicles in conformity with the finer pigment particles.

5

To illustrate our explanation, we will use the sketches below.
(Dots represent **proportionate size and number** of pigment particles within a set area. Spaces between dots represent binder (resin).)

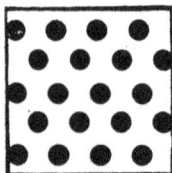

Top View

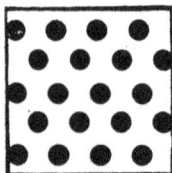

Side View

FIG. 1   MAGNIFIED PROTOTYPE PARTICLES

Coarse and few—
producing a thick
and rough surface.

PIGMENT

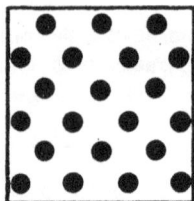

Top View

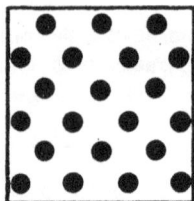

Side View

FIG. 2   MAGNIFIED PROTOTYPE PARTICLES
WITH THINNER ADDED

Same coarse particles as Fig. 1 only *farther apart.*

Increased volume covers larger area with greater d-i-s-t-a-n-c-e between particles, causing *loss of hiding power* (opacity).

**THINNER &
PIGMENT**

But the coating is no thinner, as the size of pigment particles remains the same, and because the soluble binder (resin) has been diluted, the paint will not adhere to the surface as well.

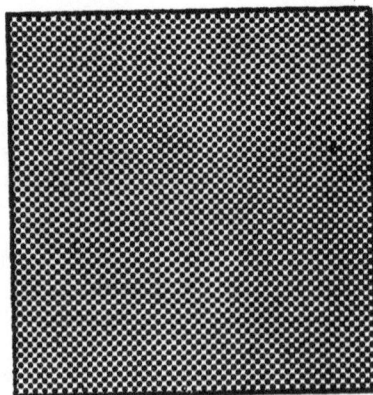

Top View

Side View

FIG. 3   MAGNIFIED MINIATURE
PARTICLES:

When finer miniature particles are used the paint film is thinner, and it will spread out over an area 4-6 times as large.

CONCLUSION:

Our experiment has shown us that by thinning protoype (or **any other paint**), **we lose more than we gain.**

GAIN	LOSS
Larger Coverage	No decrease in thickness Reduced hiding power Reduced adhesion

Our deduction shows that YOU CANNOT CHANGE PROTOTYPE PAINT INTO MINIATURE PAINT BY THINNING!

Common paint, thinned or not, is too coarse for use on *miniatures* (Fig. 1).

The addition of thinner increases coverage but only by sacrificing hiding power (opacity) and adhesion (Fig. 2).

But miniature paint provides a thin, to-scale coating with a smooth surface (Fig. 3).

Miniature paint has greater hiding power, covers more surface (**4 - 6 times**) and consequently is more *economical* in use (Fig. 3),

leaving us in no doubt that

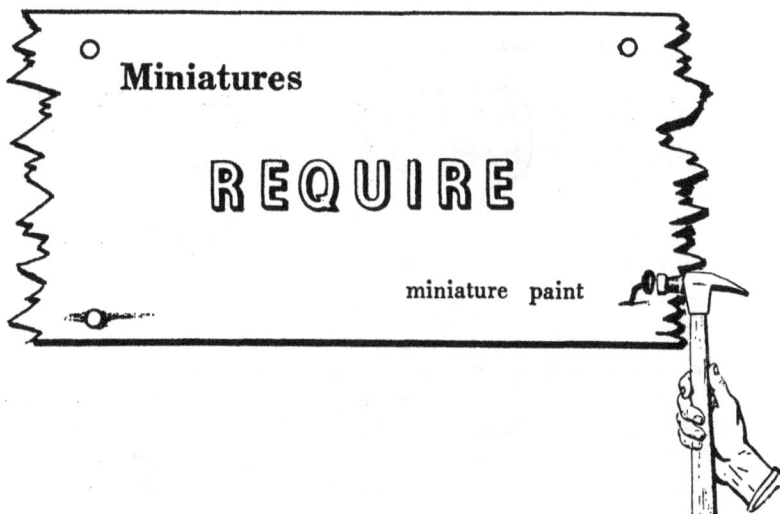

Miniatures REQUIRE miniature paint

3. Choosing Your Paint

A modelers most critical moment comes when, after hours of pains-taking construction, he has built his model—accurate in every detail—and faces

"OPERATION APPEARANCE" — *The Finishing Touch.*

It is this project that tranforms a mechancially completed but lifeless model into a *realistic miniature.* This is also the decisive moment to

STOP LOOK and SELECT the paint that will produce a *permanent* finish—requiring a *minimum* of *touch-up.*

THE PERFECT MODEL DESERVES THE PERFECT FINISH!

At this point, the modeler cannot afford to be negligent about the finishing coat by using paints which are unsuited for *miniature* work because:

A MODEL IS NO BETTER THAN THE FINISH THAT COVERS IT.

So make your choice and Face the Consequences!

The following directions can be applied in a general way to most paints. However, as each paint has its own characteristics for performance and handling, due to differences in ingredients, it would, of course, be im-possible to furnish *detailed* information on all paints. We must, for this reason, confine ourselves to supply specific information about one product only, the product we know best, have manufactured for more than 20 years, and is

SELECTED BY THE BEST AS THE BEST

Floquil Miniature Colors

FLOQUIL MINIATURE COLORS are manufactured and presented under two different labels—FLOQUIL MODEL RAILROAD COLORS and FLO-PAQUE COLORS for arts and crafts. Both groups are identical and can be substituted for each other. See comparison chart, page 11.

ALL FLOQUIL AND FLO-PAQUE COLORS:

— are *miniature paints.*
— will produce a smooth, thin, skin-tight coating—as thin as metal plating (.0002″)—and just as tough when thoroughly dry.
— will not obscure the finest surface details.
— flow on easily without struggle and "blobs."
— cover 4 - 6 times more surface than any other paint.
— will adhere to any surface: wood, metal, plastic (including styrenes), fabric, plaster, cardboard, glass, etc.
— dry to the touch in 2 - 5 minutes.
— will not crack, peel, chip or blister.
— are water and weatherproof—permanent indoors and outdoors.
— can be applied by any method: brush, airbrush, disposable propellant can, spray gun (regular or vacuum cleaner attachment), dipping, wiping, etc.—briefly, *any* method that suits you.

The two color groups (FMC and Flo-Paque Colors) furnish a full range of more than 60 intermixable, miniature colors which together with all needed accessories (coatings, etc.), provide the modeler with the most complete color group available and enable him to meet *any* challenge he may experience in painting his model equipment and scenery.

ALL FLOQUIL COLORS ARE THOROUGHLY TESTED. WE MAKE NO CLAIM WITHOUT IT HAVING BEEN PROVED. THEREFORE—EVERY FLOQUIL PRODUCT CARRIES A MONEY-BACK GUARANTEE.

COLOR GROUPS

● FLOQUIL MODEL RAILROAD COLORS
● FLO-PAQUE, FLO-GLO (DAYLIGHT FLUORESCENT), FLO-GILT (METALLIC) COLORS FOR ARTS AND CRAFTS
● FLO-STAINS

Note: FLO-GLO Colors should be used on a white surface or undercoated with White. Most effective when *outlined* with Black. Lightfast for indoor uses—show slight fading when exposed to strong sunlight over long periods of time. Applying a gloss coating to Flo-Glo Colors will prolong their life but at the same time reduce their brilliance.

Flo-Glo Colors are perfect for realistic effects on scenery (gas station banners, signs, on windows to simulate "light," etc.)

NITE-GLO is *night* luminescent. Off-white in daylight, it glows with spectral luminosity in the dark. Use on white surface or undercoat with White. For added protection, coat with a gloss coating.

FLO-STAINS: Pigmented, penetrating stains for wood or most light-colored surfaces. Easier to apply (wipe or brush on), fast drying, permanent, non-fading, require no waxing. (If used on plastic, test first.) Available in 10 wood finishes: CHERRY, MAHOGANY, OAK, WALNUT, FRUITWOOD, NATURAL PINE, DRIFTWOOD, MAPLE, SILVER SPRUCE BLUE, SCOTCH PINE GREEN.

FOUNDATION: A light buff Flo-Paque Color used as undercoating for Stains on non-wood surfaces or to block-out dark surfaces in preparation for a light stain. For instance—to change an original dark finish to a light one.

ACCESSORY PREPARATIONS AND COATINGS

The below listed accessory preparations can be used with all Floquil Color groups:

Glaze: Amber colored, medium gloss coating. For indoor and outdoor use. Quick drying (15-20 minutes appr.). Resistant to water, alcohol and most common chemicals. Dielectric. Also used for priming and to produce an eggshell finish when mixed with FMC.

Hi-Gloss: Light amber colored coating. For indoor use. Heat, water and alcohol resistant. Drying time approximately 4 hours. Produces a high gloss.

Crystal-Cote: Water-clear, glossy, quick drying coating and fixative. For indoor and outdoor use. Does not yellow. Durable. Resists abrasion and most common chemicals (except alcohol).

Aqua-Cote: Translucent, pearlescent coating. Adds realistic "moist" effect when applied over or mixed with colors portraying water. Drying time—approximately 24 hours.

Metal Conditioner and Track Cleaner: Removes grease and rust, leaves a chemically clean, dry, etched surface assuring perfect adhesion of FMC. Perfect for track cleaning. Destroys rusting agents, etc. Follow directions on label. Do not use on or with plastic.

Dio-Sol: The only chemically compatible solvent for FMC. Used for thinning, mixing, corrections, cleaning surfaces, brushes, air-brushes, etc. Use Dio-Sol generously. It is inexpensive and makes your paint go further.

Retarder: Used to slow up drying time of FMC for use with air-brush application, large surfaces, etc.

NOTICE: Different brands of paint are made with different ingredients (solvents, glazes, etc.) and *should not be mixed.* Use only thinners and coatings of the same group or as recommended by the manufacturer. Do NOT use turpentine, mineral spirits, alcohol, acetone, kerosene, gasoline, lighter fluid, etc. with FMC.

All FMC and Accessory Preparations are inflammable in their liquid state. Contain petroleum distillates. Vapor harmful. Use with adequate ventilation. Avoid prolonged contact with skin. Harmful or fatal if swallowed. Do not induce vomiting. Call physician immediately. Keep out of reach of children. Inflammable mixture. Do not use near fire or open flame. C of A 1286.

COMPARISON CHART

FLO-PAQUE COLORS and FLOQUIL MODEL RAILROAD COLORS are identical and can be substituted for each other.

REGULAR COLORS

FLO-PAQUE	RR COLORS
Antique White	
Beige	Earth
Black	Engine Black x
Blue, Dk.	RR D. Blue
Blue, Med.	RR L. Blue
Blue, Sky	
Brown	
Burnt Umber	
Chartreuse	
China*	Mud
Congo*	Roof Brown
Coral	
Dresden*	
Flesh*	Flesh
Foundation	
Gray	Reefer Gray
Green, Dk.	RR D. Green
Henna	Boxcar Red x
Leaf	RR L. Green
Lilac	
Magenta	
Maroon	RR Maroon
Olive	Depot Olive
Orange	Reefer Orange
Paris Green	
Purple	RR Purple
Red	Caboose Red
Rose	
Samoa*	
Sandstone	Concrete
Terra-Cotta	Rust
Turquoise	Jade Green
Violet	
White	Reefer White
Yellow	Reefer Yellow
* Skin Tones	Coach Green
	Grimy Black x
	Grime
	RR Primer x
	Pullman Green
	Tuscan
	Weathered Blk.
	Inst. Weath. x

METALLICS

FLO-GILT	RR COLORS
Antique Bronze	Antique Bronze
Brass	Brass
Copper	Copper
Gold, Bright	Gold, Bright
Gold, Old	
Gun Metal	Gun Metal
Patina	
Silver, Bright	Silver, Bright
Silver, Old	
Blue Gilt	
Burgundy Gilt	
Green Gilt	
Red Gilt	
Rose Gilt	
Black Gold Gilt	
Black Silver Gilt	
White Gold Gilt	
White Silver Gilt	

FLO-GLO DAYLIGHT FLUORESCENT COLORS

Cerise	
Citron	
Green	
Orange	
Yellow	
Nite-Glo	

ACCESSORIES AND COATINGS

FLO-PAQUE	RR COLORS
Al-Pro-Cote	Hi-Gloss
Crystal-Cote	Crystal-Cote
Flo-Frost	Dust
Flo-Pearl	Aqua-Cote
Glaze	Glaze
	Metal Cond.
Opalescent	
Dio-Sol	Dio-Sol
Retarder	Retarder

x Available in Aerosol Cans

11

4. Handling Colors

(BLENDING, THINNING, CONCENTRATING, RETARDING)

Just as an architect must know the raw materials going into his construction before putting his plans on the drawing paper, so a modeler should be acquainted with his paints and applicators as well as the physical characteristics of the various surfaces before he can start to use these colors effectively.

Painting will become more interesting and alive and your paints will give you better service and satisfaction when you know how to handle and control them.

BLENDING

FMC are easily intermixed (blended) to practically any shade, or thinned and retarded to any consistency and drying time needed. They are easier to handle than oil or other colors and more durable and economical.

On page 5 we have explained our ABC of *paints*. Color *blending* also has its ABC, making it possible to blend your colors to order according to your requirements by following simple rules. Our color ABC is:

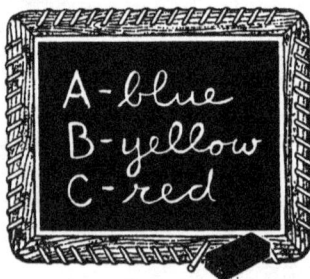

These three colors are called *primary colors* and any two or more of these can produce practically any color and shading through blending:

A+B	= GREEN
B+C	= ORANGE
A+C	= VIOLET
A+B+C	= BROWN
B+C+Black	= BROWN

As a rule, when blending colors, start with the lightest colors and add darker ones until you have the color you want. To lighten a dark color, add White or other suitable light color. To darken, add Black.

This is the simple principle for color blending and at this point it is enough information to start you off on your own experimenting.

NOTE ON LIGHTING: Where model railroads are operated in poor light, detail will show up better when colors are lightened by adding from 10-40% White. Reefer Yellow, together with White, may be used with Pullman or Coach Green. Percentages will vary with your light source, area it covers, etc.

 To work with *miniature* colors, you only need *miniature* quantities. A convenient, small unit for easy measuring is THE DROP. The drop is, of course, not a 100% exact unit but by dispersing fairly uniform size drops, we can, nevertheless, use this method as a guide with smaller quantities, allowing for some adjustments when larger amounts are blended.

You can make your own formulas by counting the number of drops of the colors and ingredients going into your mixtures and *KEEP A RECORD.*

1. Use an ordinary eye dropper (pipette) preferably with a small 1/16″ opening (appr.).
2. Count number of drops of each color or other ingredients going into your mixture. Keep *exact record* of these.
3. For each drop added, stir mixture until desired color is reached.
4. Clean eye dropper thoroughly with Dio-Sol between colors (to avoid color contamination) or have several eye droppers but with *same size* opening.

EXAMPLE #1:

You can convert your record into percentages which will enable you to duplicate colors or make larger or smaller quantities as needed—for instance, to make a light orange:

WHITE	18	drops
YELLOW	11	"
RED	8	"
GLAZE	4	"
RETARDER	2	"

Total   43 drops

Divide total number of drops (here 43) into 100 to get your percentage factor:

$$100 \div 43 = 2.325$$

13

Now multiply number of drops of each color (Column 1) with percentage factor in Column 2 to get your ratio in percentage (Column 3).

COLOR	1 NO. OF DROPS		2 MULTIPL. BY FACTOR		3 RATIO IN %
WHITE	18	×	2.325	=	41.85
YELLOW	11	×	2.325	=	25.59
RED	8	×	2.325	=	18.60
GLAZE	4	×	2.325	=	9.30
RETARDER	2	×	2.325	=	4.65
Total	43 drops			=	99.99 or 100%

To couple the drop method to a conventional system, we have found, by measurements, that a U.S. fluid ounce is made up of 1200 drops (appr.).

CONVERSION TABLE

1-oz.	=	1200 drops	
1/2-oz.	=	600 "	
1/4-oz.	=	300 "	
1/6-oz.	=	200 "	= 1 teaspoon
1/8-oz.	=	150 "	
1/16-oz.	=	75 "	

Floquil's "one ounce" bottle measures and is filled with 1-1/8 ounces or 1350 drops.

EXAMPLE #2:

Should you want to make a larger quantity of this mixture—1-1/2-ozs., for instance, you can convert the 1-1/2 ounces into drops:

1-oz.   =   1200 drops
1/2-oz.   =   600   "
1-1/2-ozs. = 1800 drops = 100% (18 drops = 1%)

COLOR	1% (18) ×	Ratio In % =	Total No. of drops=	Drops Converted Into Ounces and Drops
WHITE	18 ×	41.85 =	753.3=	1/2-oz.+1/8-oz.+ 3.3 drops
YELLOW	18 ×	25.59 =	460.6=	1/4-oz.+1/8-oz.+10.6 "
RED	18 ×	18.60 =	334.8=	1/4-oz.+34.8 "
GLAZE	18 ×	9.30 =	167.4=	1/8-oz.+17.4 "
RETARDER	18 ×	4.65 =	83.7=	1/16-oz.+8.7 "
		99.99% =	1799.8	
Total		or 1800 drops=		1-1/2 ounces

14

Rematching can be eliminated by making up larger quantities than will be used on a project and storing the "left-overs" in clean containers (bottles) with *tight* closures.

A book published by William K. Walthers, Inc., called "Railroad Color Index and Paint Mixing" can be an invaluable aid to the modeler as it tells what color to paint cars and gives the formula for mixing the color. This book should be a part of every library.

THINNING

Due to their high pigmentation, FMC are unmatched for opacity (hiding power). Simultaneously, they are unusually light in consistency (viscosity), which makes them easier to handle and adaptable for any application method.

For general uses, the colors should be used direct from the bottle. If they appear too heavy for a particular purpose, add small amounts of Dio-Sol. If large amounts of Dio-Sol are needed (for large surfaces, air-brush, etc.), add 5-10% Glaze, to compensate for the diluted resins (to preserve adhesion).

CONCENTRATING

To *increase* the pigment proportion:

1. Let pigment settle to bottom of bottle.
2. Remove small amount of clear vehicle from top with eye-dropper. Do not remove too much vehicle as too high a concentration might cause cracking on flexible surfaces.
3. Stir remaining pigment and vehicle together.

RETARDING

Retarder is used to *slow up* the drying time of FMC when required, for instance, for air-brush or large surfaces, etc. Mix Retarder with FMC in small amounts (start with 2-5% Retarder; add more if needed).

GLOSS FINISHES

1. Before using any gloss finish make SURE base coat is THOROUGHLY dry, (allow 48 hours on porous surfaces; one week on non-porous surfaces).
2. Work in a dust-free area. Protect model from dust during drying.
3. Apply gloss finish with soft brush, lint-free cloth or clean velour powder puff. F-L-O-W finish on in light strokes going in one direction only. NEVER "scrub" in. If bubbles appear, brush out with tip of brush moistened in Dio-Sol.

LIGHT GLOSS: Buff with soft cloth when throughly dry (see above).
EGGSHELL: Add approximately 5% Glaze to colors.
MEDIUM GLOSS: Use GLAZE (see above).
HIGH GLOSS: Use HI-GLOSS (see above).

5. Surfaces

REMEMBER —

"A COATING IS NEVER MORE DURABLE THAN THE SURFACE IT IS APPLIED TO!"

Old coatings or films that prevent FMC from making *direct* contact with the prime surface must be removed.

Surfaces fall into two main categories:

POROUS   and   *NON-POROUS*

POROUS SURFACES:

Porous Surfaces are: Paper, Cardboard, Plaster, Wood, Masonite, Self-hardening Clays, Fabrics, etc.

Porous Surfaces have numerous pores or openings into which FMC readily flow to establish firm anchorage. As a rule, very little preparation is required. (Old flaked and blistered coats must be removed before applying FMC.)

PLASTER OF PARIS: Plaster is one of the modelmakers' most used materials in scenery building. However, plaster of paris is of an extremely porous, loose consistency that often cracks and breaks, and plaster presents a difficult surface for *permanent* painting and staining with many ordinary paints and stains. As a coating is never more durable than the surface it is applied to, it would be negligence to invite future repairs, touch-ups and other inconveniences by *not* trying to prevent this.

There are several materials, as well as methods, that can be used to impregnate the plaster, ranging from glue water to various special preparations.

The simplest method, we believe, is to impregnate the plaster of paris with a mixture consisting of 30% Glaze with 70% Dio-Sol (appr.). This mixture penetrates deeply into the plaster of paris and, as it dries, cements the loose particles together into a firm, waterproof ceramic-like shell that resists the effects of the atmospheric variations (temperature and humidity), generally the main causes for the cracking of plaster of paris.

Furthermore, this surface takes stains and paints easily and *permanently*.

16

Procedure:

1. Let plaster construction dry thoroughly 1-2 weeks. Repair cracks occurring during this period. (We have found Textolite very good for this.)
2. Mix Glaze with Dio-Sol (use your old used Dio-Sol), 30% Glaze - 70% Dio-Sol (appr.).
3. Apply two or more coatings, one after another without waiting.
4. Let dry for 1-2 weeks before painting or staining.

Plaster impregnated this way and painted or stained with FMC is stronger, more realistic looking and will require *less upkeep*.

PLASTER SURFACE DEEPLY PENETRATED BY DIO-SOL & GLAZE.

Linseed oil, turpentine, shellac and some other *natural* resins are subject to variations in the atmospheric condition.

Paints using linseed oil and turpentine or other heavy vehicles lack the deep, penetrating features of Dio-Sol and are unable to penetrate deep enough into the plaster and carry their resins with them.

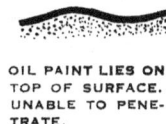

OIL PAINT LIES ON TOP OF SURFACE. UNABLE TO PENETRATE.

PAPIER MACHE: Use same procedure as for Plaster of Paris.

WOOD:

Procedure:

1. Remove all tool marks by sanding, gradually using finer grades of sandpaper. Finish with fine steel wool. (Sand *with* the grain only.)
2. Blow dust off surface.
3. Wipe surface with cloth moistened with Dio-Sol. Let dry.
4. Apply FMC or stain. Wipe or brush *with* the grain.

Models requiring a very smooth finish can be *primed* with a coating of Glaze and Dio-Sol mixed half and half. Sand smooth when bone dry (1 - 2 weeks) with fine sandpaper.

NON-POROUS SURFACES:

Non-porous surfaces are: Metals, Metal Alloys, Glass, Plastics*, etc.

Non-porous surfaces, in contrast to porous surfaces, are slick and without pits into which FMC can penetrate and "cling." FMC will, however, form a firm bond, even with slick surfaces, if these are first thoroughly cleaned with Dio-Sol.

After FMC has been applied to a non-porous surface, a longer "setting" period should be allowed BEFORE applying Glaze or other coatings (one week or more).

---

*Styrene plastics should NOT be cleaned with Dio-Sol. See Plastic (Styrene) page 18.

METAL, METAL ALLOYS: Clean (degrease) surface thoroughly with Dio-Sol. To increase adhesion to metal or metal alloy surfaces such as lead, tin, zinc, zamac, brass, bronze, etc., several procedures can be used:

1. Prime surface with half and half mixture of Glaze and Dio-Sol. Let dry 1 week. Apply paint.

OR

2. Apply Primer. Let dry for 1 week. Apply paint.

OR

3. Roughen surface gently with fine steel wool. Clean with Dio-Sol. Apply paint.

OR

4. Brush on generous amounts of Floquil Metal Conditioner, following label directions. The Metal Conditioner will leave a chemically clean, dry, etched surface, assuring perfect adhesion of FMC. (Do not use on plastic, galvanized iron, plated metals.) Apply paint. *Never* soak metal in Metal Conditioner.

Any of these methods will give good results.

Note: Sharp edges or corners (90°) should be coated several times to prevent metal from wearing through.

PLASTIC (STYRENE):

FMC are excellent for most plastics, and any method of application may be used.

Styrenes (polystyrene, etc.) are a group of plastics with a different reaction to FMC than other plastics, and therefore require a special technique in application. (Styrenes are widely used for many kinds of Model Railroad cars and scenery. Objects molded of this material are easy to recognize by their almost metallic sound when struck.) To prevent mishaps, test FMC first before applying to any plastic surface.

FMC has a temporary dissolving action on the styrene surface. This feature is one of FMC's numerous advantages over other plastic paints, as when dry, FMC has fused with the styrene and adds to the realistic effect of the finished object without hiding any of the finely molded details.

Procedure:

1. Styrene plastics should NOT be cleaned with Dio-Sol.

2. Do not remove casting bar from model parts. It serves as a handy handle while priming parts.

3. Clean molding lines, irregularities, etc. with knife, file or sandpaper while casting bar is attached to parts.

4. Use a good grade brush moderately loaded, and prime parts with FMC Primer or Foundation, using featherlight, rapid strokes with tip or edge of brush only. Do not go back over painted area.

5. Let dry 1 week.
   This coat forms permanent bond with the styrene surface and acts as barrier and base for finishing coatings. Should a few cracks appear in prime coat during drying, disregard them as they disappear after final coat is applied.

6. Separate casting bar from parts and apply final painting. No fine surface detail is lost (due to FMC's extremely thin coating).

After FMC has set completely (one week or more), its characteristic of becoming insoluble in its own solvent is transferred to the styrene and it is then possible to add new FMC.

Note: Avoid painting the edges to be cemented together with "styrene cement." Should you, by accident, have covered these edges, either remove paint (by scratching with knife, file, etc.) or use Duco or similar cements. Your model is now ready for assembly and final touch-ups.

Never use Glaze, Hi-Gloss, Aqua-Cote, Crystal Cote, Dio-Sol, Retarder or Flo-Stains directly on styrene.

AIR-BRUSH APPLICATION: See page 23.

6. Application Methods

Most modelers develop their own methods and techniques after having acquired the "touch" of FMC. For this reason, our directions can be regarded as an outline to be followed until the modeler has found his own solution more to his own liking, as FMC can be applied by ANY method to ANY surface of ANY size.

A few of the most commonly used methods are: Brush - Air-brush - Dipping - Pen (ruling pen) - Wiping - Stencil - etc.

BRUSHES

We have already described features and requirements of miniature paint, but even the best of paints is of very little value without the proper applicator. Miniature painting is painstaking, fine work and for the best results, you must use good brushes, suitable for miniature painting. It is important, therefore, to know what to look for and what to avoid when selecting brushes to apply your miniature paint.

The importance of selecting *to-scale brushes* becomes evident if you imagine yourself as a Gulliver trying to paint Lilliput engines and cars with Gulliver-scale brushes.

 At this point, we believe it would be appropriate to offer this suggestion. In dealing with miniatures, we not only have tools and materials which enable us to work with miniatures but we must imagine ourselves, do our thinking and solve our problems as Lilliputians—IN MINIATURE. Difficult problems in our Gulliver-scale world might explain themselves and suggest a Lilliput-scale solution.

The closest we can get to brushes of Lilliput-scale is good quality artists brushes (watercolor brushes).

All brushes are constructed from numerous animal hairs. For our specific use, we must look for brushes made with strong, springy shafts and fine, pointed flexible ends. (FMC will not harm the finest of brushes).

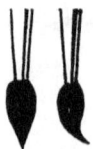

THIS

NOT THIS

20

BRUSH APPLICATION:

1. Clean all surfaces (except styrenes) with Dio-Sol and lintfree cloth.
2. Dip brush in FMC to about halfway of hair only.
3. Use tip or edge of appropriate size bush—allow colors to f-l-o-w on with long strokes and in one direction only.
4. Let object dry.
5. Clean brushes thoroughly and immediately in Dio-Sol after use. Wipe off gently on clean cloth.
6. Moisten brush in water and "shape" to point or edge. Let dry in this shape. Store away carefully.

SPRAYING

For a long time, artists have used spray application, using a simple tool which consists of two pieces of fine metal tubing placed at a 90° angle to each other. By inserting the end of one tube into a liquid (for instance, a bottle with paint) and by blowing through the other tube, liquid in the bottle rises up through the inserted tube and the jet stream from the other tube disperses it into droplets. This briefly explains jet spraying in principle.

Paint application by spraying is probably today's most popular and fastest growing method for painting models. But despite the fact that the air-brush equipment—in the long run—is the *best*, as well as the *most economical*, beginners are inclined to shy away from the seemingly high initial investment. A summary of available spray applications might be of help in selecting this equipment.

The pressure can is based on the principle shown above and has push button valves to release and shut off the propellant but has *no control* of *degree* of *pressure, shape* and *size* of the *spray cone*. The paint comes pre-mixed in the can so no blending or matching of color is possible.

A newer version of the spray can is the disposable propellant can with the propellant in one separate pressure can and a glass jar attachment for the paint. This arrangement lets the user choose his own paint and also makes it possible to mix and match colors, but otherwise has the same shortcomings as the spray can.

From tests made, we have found that the spray can and similar items (electric vibro-sprayers, vacuum cleaner attachments, etc.) have their place and can be used for covering large areas and overall painting but they are not suited for fine detail work. The Floquil Spray Can has an adjustable spray valve permitting fine, medium and heavy color application. However, even this refinement does not permit pressure regulation or give absolute control over the shape of the spray cone. Only the air-brush, a precision-made, craftsman's tool is ideally suited for the exacting detail work necessary when painting a perfect model. Practically every professional builder uses the air-brush and the many non-professionals who have air-brushes confirm our findings and are in agreement with us.

We believe that the serious, discriminating, up to date modeler should consider air-brush equipment as *one of his most needed tools*. We also feel that by pointing out its necessity, we have given the modeler good, sound advice and know that his initial investment in permanent, quality equipment will more than pay for itself in more professional-looking models, greater satisfaction and economy. As we said about Brushes, the best of paint is of little value unless you use the proper applicator. There are so many makes and models (domestic and imported) of air-brushes available today that it is impossible for us to cover them all here. Unless you are fully familiar with this type of equipment, we strongly recommend that you discuss the matter with a reliable artist supply (or model supply) dealer. Most large artist material supply houses stock various types of air-brush equipment in a wide price range. As a general rule, they are "experts" as they service the equipment they sell and their advice will be invaluable to you when making the final selection of the type and model most suited to your needs.

The main features of the air-brush:

1. It is a miniature spray gun.
2. It furnishes all the controls needed for miniature painting.
3. It allows mixing for color matching.
4. Beginners can, with short practice, obtain satisfactory results.
5. It is indispensable for scenery painting. weathering, etc.
6. It is a *one-time investment*—handles *all* colors and mixtures.

The air-brush requires a supply of compressed gas (air). To provide this has been the major expense of the equipment until recently. A good motor driven, non-pulsating compressor is not inexpensive nor is the heavy cylinder tank with gauge and control valve.

Motor driven compressors are available from about $50 to $150.

Heavy cylinder pressure tanks with gauge and control valve cost in the environment of $30-$40. Refill of tank, $3.00-$4.00.

Air-brush manufacturers, realizing this handicap, have recently introduced inexpensive adapters that fit the propellant containers. This reduces the initial investment in air-brush equipment to within most modelers' purchasing range. The adapter has a simple valve control (but no gauge) which permits the user to adjust the air pressure. Cost of adapter with one propellant unit, appr. $5.00—propellant refills, $1.75-$2.00 appr.

In our search for an inexpensive supply of compressed air (compressor) we experimented with the garden variety tank type sprayer—cost appr.

$15 (mail order house) to which we attached an air pressure regulator and gauge—cost appr. $9 (m.o.h.) and with less than 50¢ worth of fittings, converted the tank into a hand operated air compressor to which we attached an air-brush. The result is perfect, and our unit is in constant use as a portable compressor. This inexpensive equipment works as well as the best of motor driven compressors. The equipment requires a minimum of adaptation and will furnish a reasonable supply of non-pulsating air on an occasional charge from the built-in hand pump.* It should not, of course, be interpreted that this equipment will be able to handle large quantities or heavy work.

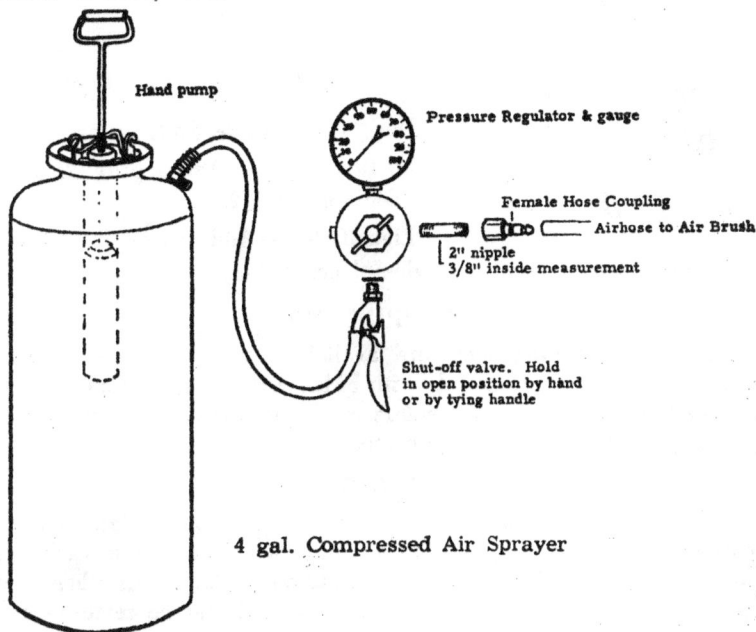

Hand pump

Pressure Regulator & gauge

Female Hose Coupling

Airhose to Air Brush

2" nipple
3/8" inside measurement

Shut-off valve. Hold
in open position by hand
or by tying handle

4 gal. Compressed Air Sprayer

AIR-BRUSH APPLICATION:
1. Clean all surfaces (except styrenes) with Dio-Sol and lintfree cloth.
2. Dilute FMC, approximate proportions: Color 75%, Glaze 5%, Dio-Sol 20%.
3. Use fine mist—low air pressure. Start with 8-10 lbs. Increase or decrease pressure as needed. Mist should reach surface just before droplets dry. Adjust the distance of your hand by tests.
4. Move air-brush parallel with surface for even distance. Do not swivel from wrist.
5. Do not try to cover surface in one coat. Avoid getting surface too wet, to avoid runs.
6. Move jet over surface making a spatter pattern. Repeat, with a short pause between coatings, until surface is completely coated.
7. Clean equipment in Dio-Sol immediately after use.

*We fill tank to 50 lbs. pressure—then reset pressure gauge to pressure needed.

DIPPING

It is often easier to dip small parts than trying to reach inaccessible crevices by brush. Attach parts to length of wire, dip, shake off and hang to dry. Suggested proportions: 65% FMC — 30% Dio-Sol — 5% Glaze.

WIPING

Wiping is a simple process often used with staining, for scenery, "weathering" railroad equipment, etc. Dip cloth or piece of felt or other applicator in colors or stain, then wipe on with a very light touch or apply diluted color or stain with brush and wipe with clean, lintfree cloth, leaving color in crevices.

STRIPING

PEN OR RULING PEN:

Dark Colors—Use FMC as prepared.

Medium Colors—Add approx. 25-30 drops of Dio-Sol per 1/2-oz.

Light Colors—Add approx. 50-55 drops of Dio-Sol per 1/2-oz.

STRIPING TOOL:

Inexpensive striping tools are available with various width striping wheels. These work excellently with FMC. Insert a small wad of cotton in the nozzle of tool (before the colors reach the wheel) to retard the flow of the colors. Change the wad with each new color.

MASKING TAPE:

The use of masking tape makes many paint jobs easier. It is an indispensable help when applying two different colors next to each other—for striping, etc. It is also handy to mask out certain areas when applying colors with spray applicators. Masking tape should be removed as soon as possible after painting.

BAKING

Baking is not needed with FMC. However, "setting" can be speeded up by "baking" model with infra-red bulb placed 8 - 10 inches from object for 20 - 30 minutes or bake in oven at 200° - 250° F for about 30 minutes. Do not bake wood or plastic.

DECAL APPLICATION

Decals stick best on semi-gloss surface. We recommend mixing Glaze with FMC as follows: For brushing—1 part Glaze to 8 parts Color. For spraying—1 part Glaze to 4 parts Color. Retarder may also be used to slow drying time and give a smooth, even finish. For complete instructions on professional decaling, refer to *Reference Manual for Model Railroaders*, published by Wm. K. Walthers, Inc., 1245 N. Water St., Milwaukee 2, Wisc.

7. Stains or Washes

FMC can be made into stains (washes) for scenery, "weathering" of models, woodwork, etc.

Mix in the following proportions:

FMC	10-30%)	
Dio-Sol	60%)	all appr.
Glaze	5-10%)	

Stir mixture well before and during use.

Thorough preparation of the surface is the only guarantee for perfect results.

APPLICATION OF WASHES AND FLO-STAINS ON WOOD:

1. Use medium fine sandpaper; sand wood to a smooth finish. Finish with fine sandpaper following the grain *only*. After sanding, remove all dust by wiping with a clean cloth. Blow clean.

2. Wipe entire surface with lintfree cloth moistened with Dio-Sol. (Does not raise grain.)

3. With brush or cloth, apply stain or wash in *long strokes following the grain*. If color appears too light, repeat application; if too dark, wipe with a Dio-Sol moistened cloth.

4. For medium gloss and a waxed-appearing surface, moisten lintfree cloth with Glaze and apply to surface. Repeat operation until cloth and surface feel "tacky" while wiping.

5. Wipe surface with cloth moistened with Dio-Sol. Permit object to dry.

6. For higher gloss, use Hi-Gloss instead of Glaze.

FLO-STAIN or washes can be applied over surfaces other than wood, such as metal, most plastics, plaster of paris, etc. They should be applied over a base coat or foundation of any other FMC or coating. To simulate wood grain, use stiff brush, special graining brush or rag, and streak to obtain desired effect. On plastics, test first.

8. Weathering

At one time the aim was uniformity of coating and exact color matching, making all rolling stock look as new as if it had just left the paint shop. This trend is now changing toward more realism, with the aim of making equipment and scenery look as real and natural as it would appear in actual use.

We, who are located in Cobleskill, New York, where the D & H Railroad literally passes our door, have opportunity to observe, daily, miles of trains moving through the countryside or stopping at our railroad station. The trains are mostly freight, at times made up of more than 100 cars, of which less than 1% look clean or new. Generally, all are weather and road-worn in various degrees. Colors are faded. Dust, stain and grime from all parts of the continent have accumulated as an all-covering film, or in streaks and patches on wooden, as well as on metal cars. Metal parts are often rusty, and some cars show patches of repair, less grimy than the rest of the car.

Observing buildings along the railroad, we find this also holds true, and scenery close to the rails show the marks of weather and time, coal and roadbed dust. It all *looks real* because *it is real.*

We are inclined to favor this new trend of getting away from the spanking new look—the toy train look. Except for prize pieces intended for display cabinet or the mantelpiece, *moving model* trains (with or without scenery) should, in our opinion, look as realistically weathered as possible to give the illusion that they are real and in use, thereby setting the distinction between model railroads and toy trains. As a matter of fact, prepainted models sold in kit form, as well as ready-to-run trains, can often pass for hand-built models by adding "weathering" to their prepainted surfaces. A good weathering job might also disguise some flaw in a less perfect model, although the basic coating should be as perfect as possible.

To apply weathering is not difficult. There are no set techniques, no hard and fast rules to follow, as each car should be completely different from the next one, even if of the same type. One reason prepainted or printed carsides cannot be "weathered" in production is that "mass weathering" would produce cars looking exactly alike, which would be unnatural and unrealistic.

26

The modeler should use every opportunity to *observe* prototypes and *remember* the fading, colors, surfaces, textures, accumulations of dust (its color), areas of repair, streaks, rust, etc.

If you are a photographer, take snapshots in color or black and white; or make small, simple sketches—anything that will help to *fasten the impressions.*

FADING

The first step in "weathering" is to simulate fading.
Aging and bleaching are natural processes which take place in the exposed pigment over periods of time. Fading should, therefore, be "built in" with the paint job, *not applied after painting.*

Procedure:

To simulate fading, the authentic color for equipment or scenery should be mixed (let down) with White in proportions ranging from 30 - 40% (or more), depending on how much fading and aging is desired. The color should be applied with the same degree of care as given a display piece. When dry, apply lettering or decals.

After drying, the model is ready for weathering.

DEPOSITS (GRIME, RUST, MUD, ETC.)

Railroad equipment is "weathered" by gradual accumulation of various kinds of dust, grime and exhaust from all over the continent, mixed with rain and snow, and depositing itself wherever a surface is exposed. In contrast to "fading" which is incorporated *in* the coloring, weathering is applied *afterward,* in order to simulate the built-up processes of exposure. "Weathering," including dust and grime, must be translucent to show the original background and markings (trademarks, etc.) through the "weathering." For this reason, a "weathering" mixture should be more like a stain or wash in consistency. A good "weathering" medium is your old dirty Dio-Sol to which you can add small quantities of FMC Dust or Black. Weathering is often streaky and gathers more on prominent surfaces or surfaces facing up.

Floquil "Instant Weathering," available in aerosol cans only, is a quick, simple, inexpensive way to "weather" cars. Grayish-beige in color, "Instant Weathering" perfectly simulates deposits of road dust and dirt. It is thin enough in consistency to allow the base color and markings to show through.

Procedure:

Apply your weathering colors with any type of applicator—a piece of cloth, felt, cellulose sponge, paper, brush. Avoid uniformity or sharply defined pattern in simulating this effect.

Rust has no definite outline and the patches are irregular in shape and vary in color from a bright orange to a deep rooftop brown within the same area. Use FMC Rust (undiluted) and vary it by adding additional colors (orange, brown, black, etc.).

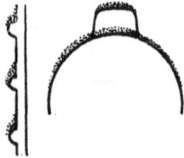

Cross section of car showing how dust settles

Rust Spot

Side of metal freight car showing deposits

The above procedures apply to cars and engines, as well as scenery, rooftops, roads, parking places, buildings, etc.

Remember, most surfaces in nature are of a flat finish except for bodies of water, etc.; also there are only few straight lines outside of strata formations. Straight lines, geometric figures and distinct definitions are generally man made.

MUD   DUST   RUST   GRIME   GRIMY BLACK

9. Hints, Suggestions, Etc.

A top ranking N.M.R.A. member once wrote us:

"Why in Heaven's name should a model builder put several long evenings into the construction of a model or building and then want to complete the finishing—the part which will be most seen—in a half-hour or so (or maybe less)?"

We are still looking for a good answer to this question.

Making models has many purposes: fun, relaxation, to while away spare time, to satisfy one's desire to create realistic, lifelike models, etc., etc. Since *whiling away time* is one of the main purposes in model making, there is no reason for speeding up any model program. Rushing generally leads to unattractive, crude models. The model maker should, at his own leisure, concentrate his effort to construct the *perfect* model—a model of which he can be proud because he has created a conversation piece, a collector's item or an object of art.

SO — DON'T TRY TO MAKE TIME — INSTEAD

TAKE YOUR TIME

GETTING READY TO PAINT

A paint project does *not* have to be messy, and messes can be eliminated if you plan and organize your project *in advance*. It is with this in mind that we suggest you have everything needed for your project ready and handy before you begin.

Procedure:

1. Select a firm, well lighted, roomy working surface.

2. Spread a layer or two of paper (newspaper or other disposable material) — just in case.

3. Have a supply of clean, lintfree cloths or paper tissue.

29

4. Have ready two small containers of Dio-Sol. Rinse brush in first container—wipe off. Rinse completely in second container—wipe off. This prevents color contamination. When first container gets too dirty, store contents in closed tin can for other uses. Dirty solvent is used for weathering, stains, grime, washes, etc., or can be mixed with Glaze for priming and impregnating plaster surfaces for scenery.

5. Place colors conveniently before you. Remove seal and stir color thoroughly. Also stir occasionally during use, particularly the metallic colors.

6. Have enough space around you for painted and unpainted pieces and for infra-red lamp if used for drying, and allow enough room to rotate item now and then during force drying. (Do NOT dry wood or plastic this way.)

Note: "Lazy Susan" bearings are available, and it is easy to make a small rotating platform on which you can place the object to be painted and thereby handle it as little as possible during finishing.

AFTER PAINTING

1. See "Brush Application" for care of brushes, page 21.

2. Clean rim of container with cloth moistened in Dio-Sol.

3. Add a few drops of Dio-Sol to color before closing.

4. Close cap *tightly*. Floquil's storage life is unlimited if air is *sealed out*.

A practical bottle for storing and mixing colors is the inexpensive Floquil Mixing Bottle (1/2-oz. capacity) packaged in carton of 6 each, complete with inner-seal caps, but any clean bottle with tight closure will serve.

Should you, after a model has been painted, change your mind and want to paint it a different color, after allowing a few days' drying time, simply paint over the old Floquil coating again with the color you now prefer. Surface details will still show up after several Floquil coatings.

MODEL RAILROADER, in its "Blue Book of Model Railroad Practices," has since December, 1957, published Diesel Color Charts and suggested formulas, two of which we have listed below transferred into percentages:

BOSTON & MAINE GP-9		
Blue:	3 parts R.R.D. Blue	60%
	2 parts Reefer White	40%
		100%

CB & Q F7		
Aluminum:	4 parts Reefer White	80%
	1 part Reefer Gray	20%
		100%

Black: Engine Black   100%
White: Reefer White   100%   Red: Caboose Red   100%

The following Diesel Color Charts have appeared in the Bluebook with suggested formulas: (for exercise, transform them into percentages)

BOSTON & MAINE GP-9—12/57
GRAND TRUNK W. GP-9—12/57

SOUTHERN F-7—1/58
ILL. CENTRAL—1/58
WABASH GP-7—2/58
NORTH. PACIFIC GP-9—2/58

CHI. & NORTHW. GP-9—3/58
WEST. MD. GP-9, 3/58

READING GP-9—4/58
CB & Q F7—4/58

GREAT NORTHERN. GP-9—5/58
NY CENT. F-7—5/58

MO. PACIF. UNIT—6/58
BESSEMER & L.E. F UNIT—6/58

C & O F UNIT—7/58
ATL. COAST GP-9—7/58

PA. F UNIT—8/58
ST. LOUIS-SAN FRAN. F UNIT—8/58

LOUISV. & NASHV. GP UNIT—9/58
DENVER & RIO G. WEST. F UNIT—9/58

UNION PAC. F UNIT—10/58
LACK. GP UNIT—10/58

WEST. PACIF GP UNIT—11/58
KANSAS C. SO. F UNIT—11/58

N. PACIF. F UNIT—1/59
CHI. & E. ILL. E UNIT—1/59

FLA. E.C. GP UNIT—2/59
B & O GP UNIT—2/59

NY, CHI. & ST. LOUIS GP—3/59
MINN., ST. P & S.S.M—3/59

ST. LOUIS-SAN FRAN. GP—4/59
CAN. NATL F—4/59

MO., K & T GP—5/59
B & O F UNIT—5/59

PA. E UNIT—6/59
C & O E UNIT—6/59

AT. COAST GP—7/59
SO. PAC. F UNIT—7/59

MO. PAC. GP—8/59
ILL. CENT. GP—8/59

PA. GP—10/59
BOSTON & ME F—10/59

GREAT NORTH F—11/59
CHI., BURL & QUINCY E—11/59

C & O F—12/59
SO. PACIF E—12/59

MINN. ST. P & SSM GP—
  (Soo Line—1/60)
SOUTH. GP—1/60
MO., K & T F.—1/60
FLA. E. C. F—1/60

UNION PAC GP—4/60
SOUTH E.—4/60

SO. PAC. GP—5/60
LOUISV. & NASH. F—5/60

WABASH F UNIT—6/60
WEST. MD F—6/60

READING F—8/60
CHI. & NW. E—8/60

SO. PACIF.—1/61
ERIE—1/61

FLA. E. C.—3/61
SANTA FE—3/61

LEHIGH V. ALCO R.S.—5/61
ST. LOUIS-SAN FRAN. EMD E—
  5/61

CHI. & ILL. MID. EMD R.S.—6/61
L. I. ALCO R.S.—6/61

ATL. C.L. EMD Y.S.—7/61
CENT. OF GA. EMD F—7/61

MILW. ROAD ALCO R.S.—8/61
NEW HAVEN FL-9—8/61

GREAT NORTH. ALCO R.S.—10/61
CB & Q EMD Y.S.—10/61

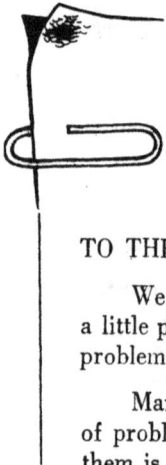

TO THE MODELER . . .

We are confident that you, with your Floquil Colors, your Manual, a little practice and your own ingenuity, will be able to solve most coloring problems confronting you.

Many inspirations, ideas and hints have come about through discussions of problems with your fellow modelers, and one of the best places to meet them is at the Model Railroad Club. If a Model Railroad Club is not conveniently located for you, start a club of your own together with some other modelers in your neighborhood. It will improve your model making and make it more interesting.

If you are not now a member of the N.M.R.A., we cannot urge you strongly enough to become one. The benefits are great—the fee is worth it. Their address is: N.M.R.A., Inc., P.O. Box 1328, Station C, Canton, Ohio 44708.

Should you, despite your best efforts, face a problem that stumps you, you can always drop us a line with a description of your problem, and if it is within our scope and ability to be of aid to you, you may depend on Floquil.

So now, face your problems—solve them as you go along and even if now and then you should make a blunder (as we all do), keep on striving for perfection. We are certain you will enjoy model railroading.

Yours for better miniature painting,

Harald Rosenlund

FLOQUIL PRODUCTS, INC.

Cobleskill, N. Y. 12043

A REVEALING PEEK INTO OUR MAIL —

THESE COMMENTS ARE SPONTANEOUS
AND UNSOLICITED AND ARE ONLY A FEW
OF THE MANY IN OUR FILES. PHOTO-
STATIC COPIES OF THESE EXCERPTS OF
LETTERS WILL BE FURNISHED ON REQUEST.

"I have a new diesel engine and Floquil Model Railroad Colors made it look *more detailed* than ever."

E.P., N.J.

"I have been in the paint manufacturing business for 17 years and appreciate the need for a special paint for small detailed articles. I know, I tried some of the paint I have at home!"

W.W.I., Mich.

"I like your Floquil Model Railroad Colors because I find it *sticks to metal better* than any other paint and it leaves a *thinner coating*."

D.N., Ill.

"I find your Floquil Model Railroad Colors excellent for old time equipment as it comes in so many different colors."

D.E.H., Wash.

"I purchased some of your railroad colors about five months ago. I was very well pleased with the way they worked . . . noticeably the silver. I have never experienced a silver paint that was *so easy to apply* and yet gave the *high quality finish* that your silver did."

O.P.D., Wash.

"Whenever painting time comes to my models, I put only Floquil products on them and I really mean it. All my models are finished that way and a goodly number of them have been *feature articles in Model Railroader*. I consider your paint, *bar none, the best available used either with brush or spray*."

R.B., Calif.

"May I take this opportunity to thank you for your wonderful Floquil Model Railroad Colors. It seems to be the *only paint* that will *stick* to my engines *without peeling*."

W.M.G., Pa.

"I can truly say that your product is by far the best that I have ever used. I custom build engines and I have found that the *one single important item is the way it looks painted*. I've tried other paints but I always come back."

H.K., Pa.

EXCERPTS FROM
UNSOLICITED LETTERS
FROM MODEL RAILROADERS
IN FOREIGN COUNTRIES —

"Two or three years ago I ordered from you some *metallic Floquil Model Railroad Colors* and they were *so splendid* that I must have some other colors also."

F.D., Basel, Switzerland

"It was recently the writer's good fortune to obtain and subseqently use a jar of *Floquil Model Railroad Colors* made especially for model railroaders and *in consequence of the results obtained* from this sample jar, it is *now desired to obtain a full range of your various colors*."

P.W.D., Victoria, Australia

"I have just finished painting an engine with your *locomotive black* (Floquil Model Railroad Colors) and would say it is an *excellent job*. I used your Railroad Colors on some boxcars last spring and the *results were just as satisfactory as on the engine*."

W.W.B., Lachine, Que., Can.

"I have just used a jar of your Floquil Model Railroad Colors on some of my models and am *very pleased* with its *powers of quick-drying, etc*."

D.A., Northumberland, Eng.

"Having used your very fine paint for these many years on all my Mountain Valley Line cars, and enjoyed every brush of it, it really is time to say thanks for such a consistently fine product."

W.R.W., North Surrey, B.C.

"I have just started using the Floquil paint products on some of my model railroad equipment. It is tops."

P.O.S., Quebec, Canada

"I am employing your products in the railroad field for at least five years now and I ever has been satisfied with them."

J.P., Congo Republic

"I have been using your paints for the last three years and have found nothing better as an overall paint for plastics, wood, or metal. Keep up the good work."

W.R.Jr., Ont., Canada